W0082667

THE BEST 50

SOUPS AND STEWS
For Slow Cooker, Stovetop,
Oven and Pressure Cooker

Sandra Rudloff

BRISTOL PUBLISHING ENTERPRISES
Hayward, California

Printed in the United States of America.

ISBN 10: 1-55867-346-6

ISBN 13: 978-1-55867-346-5

Cover design: Frank J. Paredes
Cover photography: John A. Benson
Food stylist: Susan Devaty

DIFFERENT COOKING OPTIONS
FOR SOUPS AND STEWS

The recipes in this book are divided according to the different methods of cooking. Some recipes can be cooked using more than one method, depending on time, ingredients available and convenience for the cook. **Stovetop** and **pressure cooker** recipes tend to cook more quickly; recipes for the **oven** or **slow cooker** cook more slowly.

Stovetop soups and stews contain ingredients needing more attention or having a short cooking time.

Slow cooker (or Crock-Pot®) soups and stews combine all ingredients at the beginning and cook mostly undisturbed, useful for a cook who is busy or away for the day. A slow cooker is more energy-efficient than an oven, and keeps the kitchen cooler on a hot day.

A pressure cooker is ideal for making soups and stews with tougher cuts of meat, and for saving time and fuel, especially when cooking bean-based soups and stews. This is a "no peek" method of cooking, so is only suitable for some recipes. Stovetop or slow cooker cooking options are noted at the end of these recipes.

Oven-cooked soups and stews work for larger cuts of meats and recipes that need minimal attention during cooking. They tend to cook in a shorter amount of time than in the slow cooker because the temperatures are higher.

VEGETABLE TOPPING SUGGESTIONS—CHOPPED OR SLICED

*Carrots (Blanched for 1 minute) White mushrooms
*Turnips (Blanched for 1 minute) Spinach
Pea pods   Zucchini
Red bell peppers   Chives
Green Onions   Parsley

OTHER TOPPING POSSIBILITIES

Croutons   Sour cream
Chopped hard-cooked egg   Crumbled cooked bacon
Crushed tortilla chips   Grated cheeses
Slivered almonds   Fried won ton strips
Chopped peanuts or walnuts

CHICKEN STOCK—LEGS AND THIGHS

This stock is economical to make, and the flavor is much better than canned broth. It uses chicken thighs and legs instead of a carcass from a cooked chicken. Buy frozen leg or thigh pieces, frequently sold in large bags, just for making stock. Make sure to cook the chicken until all sides are a deep golden brown.

1 chicken leg
1 chicken thigh
4 cups water
$\frac{1}{2}$ tsp. salt

1 small carrot, cut into chunks
1 stalk celery, cut into 2-inch pieces
$\frac{1}{2}$ yellow onion, thickly sliced

In a medium stockpot, brown leg and thigh over medium heat, until browned on all sides, about 20 minutes. Keep pot covered at all times except when turning chicken. Add remaining ingredients and bring to a boil. Cover, reduce heat to low and simmer for 1 hour. Pour stock through a wire strainer and discard vegetables, chicken skin and bones. Reserve chicken meat or chop and add to stock. Remove fat from top surface of stock prior to using or freezing.

CHICKEN STOCK—CARCASS

When you cook a chicken for a meal, use everything left over, including wings and legs, to give you a full-flavored stock. Cook the neck from the giblets package along with your carcass: you'll get even more flavor. All stocks and broths freeze well — you may never have to buy canned stock again.

1 chicken carcass, plus neck from giblets package
4 cups water
½ bay leaf
1 small carrot, cut into chunks

1 stalk celery, cut into 2-inch pieces
½ yellow onion, unpeeled and thickly sliced
¼ tsp. salt

Combine all ingredients in a medium stockpot and bring to a boil. Cover and reduce heat to low. Simmer for at least 2 hours, or until bones separate easily. Pour stock through a wire strainer and discard vegetables, chicken bones and skin or meat. Remove fat from top surface of stock prior to using or freezing. Refrigerate and use within 3 days, or freeze for up to 6 months.

BEEF STOCK

Making beef stock is very inexpensive. Go to your market and ask someone in the meat department for soup bones. Sometimes you'll even get them for free. You can also make this with some meaty bone from cuts such as short ribs, shank portions or back ribs if you can't purchase soup bones.

3 lb. beef soup bones
16 cups water
2 bay leaves
1 cup chopped carrots

1 cup chopped celery
1 yellow onion, chopped
$1/2$ tsp. salt

In a large stockpot, brown beef bones. Add water and all remaining ingredients and bring to a full boil. Reduce heat to low, cover and simmer for 3 hours. Pour stock through a wire strainer. Refrigerate and use within 3 days, or freeze for up to 6 months. Skim off fat before using or freezing.

FISH STOCK

Fish stock recipes often call for mostly heads, skeletons and scraps, which I rarely have. So I created this fish stock by using very inexpensive fish pieces. Fish gives up its flavor to the broth very quickly, so a long simmer time isn't needed. Also, do not use strongly-flavored fish such as salmon. Use only the mildest-tasting fish.

1 lb. mild white-fleshed fish (cod, haddock or similar)
1 yellow onion, peeled and chopped
2 stalks celery, chopped
$\frac{1}{2}$ tsp. salt
6 cups water

Cut fish into 2-inch pieces. Combine all ingredients in a medium-to-large stockpot. Bring to a boil, cover and reduce heat to low. Simmer for 30 minutes.

Pour stock through a wire strainer and press lightly to extract as much juice as possible, especially from fish pieces. Refrigerate and use within 3 days, or freeze for up to 6 months.

VEGETABLE STOCK

Vegetable stock should be fairly neutral in flavor. Strong-flavored vegetables such as broccoli or Brussels sprouts will make your stock taste primarily of that vegetable. This stock is a good substitute for chicken or fish broth.

8 cups water
1 clove garlic, chopped
2 yellow onions, chopped
4 carrots, chopped
4 stalks celery, chopped
2 russet potatoes, thickly sliced
1 cup chopped white mushrooms
1/2 tsp. salt

Combine all ingredients in a large stockpot. Bring to a boil, cover and reduce heat to low. Simmer for 1 hour. Pour stock through a wire strainer and press lightly to extract as much juice as possible. Refrigerate and use within 3 days, or freeze for up to 6 months.

ROASTED VEGETABLE STOCK

Makes about 4 quarts

This is a roasted vegetable stock. Its bolder flavor can be used as you would use beef stock.

2 yellow onions, halved
2 roma tomatoes, halved
4 carrots, cut into 2-inch pieces
4 stalks celery, cut into 2-inch pieces
2 potatoes, cut into slices
3 cloves garlic, peeled
1 cup whole white mushrooms
$1/4$ cup olive oil
16 cups water
$1/2$ tsp. salt

Heat oven to 400°. Place onions and tomatoes cut-side up in a large pan or roaster. Arrange carrots, celery, potatoes, garlic and mushrooms around onions and tomatoes. Drizzle olive oil over all vegetables. Place vegetables in oven and roast until browned, about 45 to 60 minutes.

Place vegetables and any liquid in pan into a large stockpot. (Note: If you have bits of vegetables stuck to pan, or if there are some browned juices, add 1 cup water to pan and return to oven for 10 minutes. Scrape up any bits and add liquid and vegetable bits to stockpot.) Add water and salt and bring to a boil over high heat. Reduce heat to low, cover and simmer for 1 hour.

Pour stock through a wire strainer and press lightly to extract as much juice as possible. Refrigerate and use within 3 days, or freeze for up to 6 months.

CHICKEN MINESTRONE

This is a lighter version of traditional minestrone, but with lots of the same vegetables and flavors.

6 cups chicken stock
1 cup chopped zucchini
1 cup chopped carrots
1 cup chopped fresh green beans, cut into 1/2-inch pieces
1 can (14.5 oz.) Italian-style chopped tomatoes
1 can (15 oz.) great Northern beans
2 cups shredded Napa cabbage
2 cups chopped cooked chicken
1 cup chopped banana squash
1/2 tsp. dried basil
1/2 tsp. dried oregano

Combine all ingredients in a large stockpot. Bring to a boil, reduce heat to low and simmer until all vegetables are tender, about 30 minutes.

OLD-FASHIONED CHICKEN NOODLE SOUP

Servings: 4–6

Not at all like soup from a can, this is just a simple warming soup that is perfect for a rainy day.

8 cups chicken stock
1 cup minced cooked chicken
2 carrots, minced
2 stalks celery, minced
1 cup uncooked thin egg noodles

In a large stockpot, bring chicken stock, chicken, carrots and celery to a boil. Reduce heat to low and simmer for 20 minutes.

While soup is simmering, cook noodles according to package directions. Rinse with cool water and drain. Add drained noodles to soup and serve immediately.

CHINESE CABBAGE AND NOODLE SOUP

Servings: 4–6

Asian buckwheat noodles are also called "chunka soba" and can be found in all Asian markets and many supermarkets. The shredded cabbage strands look like noodles when cooked.

6 cups chicken stock
1 tbs. soy sauce
1-inch piece fresh ginger, peeled and sliced
2 cups chopped cooked chicken
4 cups shredded Napa cabbage
1/2 lb. buckwheat noodles, cooked according to package directions

In a large stockpot, mix together stock, soy sauce, ginger and cooked chicken. Bring to a boil, cover and simmer for 10 minutes. Remove ginger pieces.

Add cabbage and noodles and cook only until cabbage is wilted. Serve immediately.

SAUSAGE AND PASTA SOUP

Feel free to use any shape pasta here. Be sure to cook the pasta "al dente", meaning slightly chewy, not overcooked. Also, don't let soup simmer too long after adding, or your pasta will be overcooked.

4 Italian sausages in casings
2 stalks celery, chopped
2 carrots, chopped
1 yellow onion, chopped

8 cups chicken stock
2 cups chopped peeled tomatoes
2 cups cooked tiny shell pasta,
   cooked "al dente"

Place sausages in a large stockpot. Cook sausages over medium heat until browned and cooked through. Remove from pot to cool slightly. Pour off excess fat from pot.

Return pot to stove. Add celery, carrots and onion and sauté until onions begin to brown. Add stock and tomatoes and bring to a boil, scraping the bottom to loosen any browned bits. Reduce heat to low, cover and simmer for 20 minutes. While soup simmers, cut sausages into ¼-inch-thick slices. Return sausage slices to soup and simmer for 10 minutes. Add cooked pasta and simmer for 5 minutes.

WINTER VEGETABLE SOUP

Servings: 6–8

You can get all the fresh vegetables for this soup easily and inex-pensively in the middle of winter.

8 cups chicken, beef or vegetable stock
$1/2$ cup chopped yellow onion
1 cup chopped celery
1 cup chopped carrots
$1/2$ cup chopped peeled turnips
1 cup chopped peeled potato
2 cups shredded green cabbage
$1/2$ tsp. salt

Combine all ingredients in a large stockpot. Bring to a boil over high heat. Cover and reduce heat to low. Simmer for 15 minutes or until potatoes are tender.

ROASTED CORN CHOWDER

Cooking the corn under the broiler give this soup a smoky taste.

6 ears corn, husked and cleaned
3 tbs. vegetable oil
3 slices bacon, chopped
1/2 yellow onion, chopped

4 cups vegetable stock or water
2 medium potatoes, peeled and
  chopped
2 cups half-and-half

Preheat broiler. Rub corn with vegetable oil and set on a cookie sheet. Place under broiler and cook until corn begins to brown, about 5 minutes. Turn ears over and brown other sides. Remove from oven and let cool. When cool, scrape off kernels. Reserve corn cobs for soup.

In a large stockpot over medium heat, brown bacon until crisp. Remove from pot and drain all fat from pot. Add onions and sauté until translucent. Add stock, potatoes, corn cobs and corn kernels. Bring to a boil and reduce heat to low. Cover and simmer for 30 minutes, or until potatoes are tender. Remove corn cobs and discard. Add half-and-half and cooked bacon to soup and serve.

BEEF AND BARLEY SOUP

Not too many people use barley anymore, but I like the chewy texture it adds to soup.

2 tbs. olive oil
1 lb. beef stew meat, cut into tiny pieces
10 cups beef stock
1/2 cup barley
2 carrots, sliced
2 turnips, peeled and chopped
2 stalks celery, chopped
1 tsp. salt

Heat oil in a large stockpot over medium-high heat. Add beef and cook until browned. Add stock, barley, carrots, turnips, celery and salt, and bring mixture to a boil. Reduce heat to low and simmer for 1 hour, until barley is done and beef is tender.

BAJA BLACK BEAN AND SHRIMP SOUP

If you think all bean soups are heavy, try this one. The fresh taste of bay shrimp and cilantro lighten the heavy bean taste.

2 cans (16 oz. each) black beans
2 stalks celery, chopped
1 green bell pepper, seeded and chopped
1 red bell pepper, seeded and chopped
5 cups chicken stock
2 cups chopped tomatoes
1 tsp. ground cumin
1/2 lb. bay shrimp
2 tbs. chopped fresh cilantro

Combine all ingredients except shrimp and cilantro in a large stockpot. Bring to a boil over medium heat. Cover, reduce heat and simmer for 30 minutes.

Stir in shrimp and cilantro. Serve immediately.

SEAFOOD SOUP

This tomato-based soup features whatever fresh fish you can find. You need about 1 1/4 lbs. of fish fillets. The fillets should be about 1/2-inch thick. Skip the shellfish for this recipe—this is meant to be an easy-to-eat soup!

1/2 lb. cod fillets
1/2 lb. red snapper fillets
1/4 lb. salmon fillets
1/2 cup olive oil
1 yellow onion, chopped
1 cup white wine

2 cups canned tomatoes, finely chopped
4 cups fish stock or water
1/2 lb. small cooked shrimp
1/2 lb. cooked crabmeat
grated zest of 1 lemon

Cut fillets into small, bite-size pieces. Heat olive oil in a large stockpot over medium heat. Add onion and sauté until golden. Add wine and bring to a boil, scraping up any browned bits on bottom of pot. Add tomatoes, stock and fish pieces. Bring to a boil. Cover, reduce heat to low, and simmer for 20 minutes. Stir in cooked shrimp, crab and lemon zest. Continue to cook until heated through.

MULLIGATAWNY SOUP

This creamy Indian soup is flavored with curry. Serve with finely chopped apples, raisins, or peanuts.

1 lb. boneless, skinless chicken breasts
2 tbs. vegetable oil
1 yellow onion, chopped
1 clove garlic, minced
5 cups chicken stock
1 tbs. curry powder, or to taste
$\frac{1}{2}$ tsp. powdered dried ginger
2 whole cloves
1 cup diced carrots
1 cup cooked white rice
1 cup heavy cream or unsweetened coconut milk

Cut chicken into tiny pieces. Heat oil in a large stockpot over medium heat. Add chicken and cook until meat is white but not browning. Add onion and garlic and continue to cook until onions are golden. Add stock, curry powder, ginger, cloves and carrots. Bring to a boil, cover and reduce heat to low. Simmer for 30 minutes. Remove cloves from soup. Add white rice to soup and heat through. Stir in cream or coconut milk and serve immediately.

HAM AND POTATO SOUP

Chunks of ham and potato are surrounded by a potato puréed soup. A great way to use up some leftover holiday ham!

6 cups water
4 large potatoes
3 cups chopped cooked ham
1 yellow onion, chopped

2 stalks celery, chopped
1 tsp. salt
2 cups milk

Place water in a large stockpot. Peel and chop 3 of the potatoes and add to water. Bring to a boil over high heat. Cover and simmer until potatoes are falling-apart tender, about 20 minutes.

Purée soup in batches and return to pot. Peel and coarsely chop remaining potato and add to pot. Add ham, onion, celery and salt. Bring to a boil over medium heat; cover and reduce heat to low. Simmer until potato chunks are tender, about 30 minutes, depending on the size of your chunks. Add milk until you reach desired thickness, and heat for another 5 minutes.

CHEDDAR CHEESE SOUP

This creamy soup can be made into a very hearty meal by adding 1 or 2 cups of chopped cooked ham just before serving. It is also wonderful when topped with some crumbled crisp bacon.

2 tbs. butter
2 tbs. flour
6 cups milk
2 cups grated sharp cheddar cheese
1/4 tsp. dry mustard

In a large stockpot, melt butter over medium heat. Add flour and, using a wire whisk, mix in until smooth. Pour milk into sauce, stirring constantly. Return to heat and cook until mixture begins to thicken, stirring constantly. Do not let milk boil. Add cheese and dry mustard and stir constantly until melted. Serve immediately.

AND SPINACH SOUP

is how my Italian grandmother used to make lentil soup. You also add some chunks of kielbasa or cooked ham to make this heartier.

2 cups lentils
8 cups water or vegetable stock
1 carrot, chopped
3 stalks celery, chopped
1 yellow onion, chopped
1 potato, peeled and chopped
1 can (14 oz.) ready-cut
tomatoes

$1/2$ tsp. dried sage
2 cloves garlic, minced
1 tsp. salt
$1/2$ lb. spinach, washed and cut
into $1/2$-inch strips

Combine all ingredients, except spinach, in a large stockpot. Bring to a boil, cover and reduce heat. Simmer until lentils are tender, about 45 minutes. Add spinach and simmer for another 5 minutes.

OLD WORLD CABBAGE SOUP

This soup is hearty and inexpensive to make. Serve with a rustic bread for an old-fashioned meal.

1 head Savoy or Napa cabbage, shredded
1 yellow onion, chopped
2 carrots, chopped
2 potatoes, peeled and chopped
6 cups chicken stock

Combine all ingredients in a large stockpot. Bring to a boil over high heat and reduce heat to low. Cover and simmer for 30 minutes, or until potatoes are tender.

CREAMY MUSHROOM SOUP

Lots of mixed mushrooms make this soup very different from canned cream of mushroom soup. My favorite wild mushrooms to use in this soup are chanterelles. This soup is very rich and filling, so it can be a main dish when served with bread and some cheeses.

1/4 cup butter
1/2 lb. white mushrooms, finely chopped
2 leeks, white part only, thinly sliced

1 lb. wild mushrooms, chopped
4 cups chicken or vegetable stock or water
1 cup heavy cream

Melt butter in a large stockpot over medium heat. Add chopped white mushrooms and sauté until liquids are released and they begin to brown. Add leeks and continue to cook until leeks are translucent.

Add wild mushrooms and stock. Bring to a boil and reduce heat to low. Simmer, uncovered, for 15 minutes. Remove from heat and add cream. Do not return to heat. Serve immediately.

CREAMY CHICKEN AND CORN SOUP

Servings: 4–6

Many Chinese restaurants offer a version of this soup. This is thicker than a chowder because of the addition of white rice. Top with a sprinkling of slivered green onions.

1 cup shredded cooked chicken
1 can (17 oz.) creamed corn
1 cup corn kernels, frozen, fresh or canned
5 cups chicken stock
½ cup uncooked white rice
1 tsp. soy sauce

Combine all ingredients in a large stockpot. Bring to a boil over medium heat, stirring frequently. Reduce heat and simmer until rice is very tender, about 30 minutes. Add additional stock if you prefer a thinner soup.

CREAM OF SPINACH SOUP

If you like creamed spinach, you'll love this soup.

3 cups chicken stock
2 medium potatoes, peeled and chopped
4 cups spinach, leaves only
2 cups half-and-half
1/2 tsp. freshly ground nutmeg

Combine chicken stock and potatoes in a large stockpot. Bring to a boil and cook until potatoes are very tender, about 20 minutes. Remove from heat and add spinach. Stir to mix, cover and let stand for 5 minutes.

Purée potatoes, spinach and cooking stock in batches. Return puréed mixture to pot and heat to boiling. Remove from heat and stir in half-and-half and nutmeg. Serve immediately. If soup is not hot enough, return to medium heat and continue to warm slowly, but never allow soup to boil. Stir frequently while heating.

RED CHICKEN CURRY

Curry and tomatoes pair up for a spicy chicken stew. Serve over hot white or brown rice for a complete meal.

2 tbs. vegetable oil
1 chicken, cut into 8 pieces
1 yellow onion, chopped
1 green bell pepper, cut into chunks
2 cans (14½ oz. each) stewed tomatoes
1 tbs. curry powder
1 tsp. garlic salt

Heat oil in a medium stockpot over medium-high heat. Add chicken and sauté until chicken is just beginning to brown, about 15 minutes. Reduce heat to medium-low.

Add onion, bell pepper, tomatoes, curry powder and garlic salt. Stir to mix and simmer for 30 minutes, or until chicken is tender.

CHICKEN EL CID

This stew gets a bright and fresh taste by adding cilantro just before serving.

2 tbs. olive oil
1 frying chicken, cut into 8 or more serving pieces
1 yellow onion, sliced
2 cloves garlic, minced
1 green bell pepper, seeded and coarsely chopped
3 cups ready-cut tomatoes
$\frac{1}{2}$ tsp. Tabasco Sauce
$\frac{1}{2}$ tsp. garlic salt
$\frac{1}{2}$ cup chopped fresh cilantro

In a large Dutch oven or stockpot, heat oil over medium heat. Add chicken and cook until browned on all sides. Add onion, garlic, bell pepper, tomatoes, Tabasco Sauce and garlic salt. Stir to mix. Reduce heat to low and simmer for 1 hour.

Remove from heat. Stir in fresh cilantro and serve immediately.

IRISH STEW

The rule of Irish stew is that you have to use lamb and potatoes — anything else is up to you. Serve with a nice crusty bread.

3 tbs. flour
1 tsp. salt
2 lb. lamb chunks, cut into
   1½-inch cubes
¼ cup vegetable oil or bacon
   drippings
1 yellow onion, coarsely chopped

3 large potatoes, peeled and cut
   into 1½-inch chunks
3 cups water
¼ tsp. dried rosemary
¼ tsp. dried thyme
1 cup baby carrots

Mix flour and salt together in a plastic bag. Add lamb chunks and shake to coat well. Over medium heat, heat oil in a Dutch oven or large stockpot. Add meat chunks and cook until browned on all sides. Add onion, potatoes, water, rosemary and thyme to pot. Scrape off any browned bits attached to bottom of pot. Bring to a boil; cover and reduce heat to low. Simmer for 1 hour, stirring occasionally. Add carrots to pot; cover and continue to cook for 30 minutes.

LAMB STEW WITH OLIVES AND ROSEMARY   Servings: 4–6

If you like their strong taste, you can use kalamata olives here instead of black olives — or try a mixture of half of each type. Roasted potatoes make a nice side dish to the flavors of this stew.

2 tbs. olive oil
2 lb. lamb stew meat
1 clove garlic, minced
$\frac{1}{2}$ tsp. dried rosemary, or 1 tsp. chopped fresh
2 cups beef stock
1 can (7 oz.) pitted black olives

In a Dutch oven or stockpot, heat oil over medium-high heat. Add lamb and garlic and sauté until browned. Add rosemary, stock and olives, and bring to a boil. Cover and reduce heat to low. Simmer for 1 hour, or until meat is tender.

CHICKEN CACCIATORE

This is a comfort food for me, especially when served with steaming hot polenta. If you prefer, serve with wide egg noodles.

1/4 cup olive oil
1 frying chicken, cut into 8 or more serving pieces
2 cloves garlic, minced
1 yellow onion, sliced
1/2 cup white wine
1 bell pepper, seeded and sliced
1/2 lb. mushrooms, sliced
2 cans (28 oz. each) plum tomatoes
1/2 tsp. dried oregano
1/2 tsp. dried basil
1/2 tsp. salt

Heat oil in a large stockpot or Dutch oven over medium heat. Add chicken and cook until golden brown. Remove chicken and set aside. Add garlic and onion to pot and sauté until onions begin to brown. Add wine and scrape up browned bits from bottom of pan.

Return chicken to pot. Add bell peppers, mushrooms, tomatoes, oregano, basil and salt and stir to mix. Reduce heat to low, cover and simmer for 45 minutes.

CHICKEN GUMBO

You can't make gumbo without okra. This can be considered both a stew —because of the large pieces of chicken — and a soup. If you don't want large pieces of chicken, you can use about 2 lb. boneless, skinless breasts or thighs, cut into chunks, instead.

2 tbs. vegetable oil
1 frying chicken, cut into 8 or
  more serving pieces
1 yellow onion, chopped
1 cup chopped tomatoes
1 cup sliced okra, about 1/2-inch
  slices

1/2 cup chopped green bell
  pepper
1/2 cup chopped celery
1 carrot, chopped
8 cups chicken stock
1/2 tsp. dried thyme
1 bay leaf

Heat oil in a large Dutch oven or stockpot over medium heat. Add chicken and cook until browned. Add onions and continue cooking until onions are lightly browned. Add all remaining ingredients and increase heat to high. Bring to a boil, reduce heat, cover and simmer for 1 hour. Remove bay leaf before serving.

HUNGARIAN PORK STEW

Pork, potatoes and cabbage make for a hearty one-pot meal.

¼ cup olive oil
3 lb. pork stew meat
1 yellow onion, sliced
1 medium head Savoy or Napa
  cabbage, coarsely shredded

3 large potatoes, peeled and cut
  into large chunks
1 cup white wine
3 cups chicken stock
1 bay leaf
1 clove garlic, peeled

Over medium heat, heat oil in a large stockpot or Dutch oven. Add pork and cook until browned. You will need to do this in batches. As meat is browned, remove to a bowl. Add onion, cabbage and potatoes to pot, stirring to coat vegetables in remaining oil. Add wine and stock and scrape up any browned bits on bottom of pan.

Return pork to pot and add bay leaf and garlic. Bring to a boil, reduce heat to low, cover and simmer for 1 hour. Remove cover. Remove bay leaf and garlic and discard. Continue to cook for an additional 30 minutes to reduce stock.

TUSCAN BEAN SOUP

Rosemary and smoked ham hocks flavor this white bean soup. Serve with some crusty French bread to dip into the soup. Spooning chopped fresh tomatoes on top makes a pretty presentation.

1 cup dried white beans, such as
  Great Northern
4 cups water
4 cups chicken stock
1 ham hock
3 cloves garlic, minced

2 tsp. chopped fresh rosemary
1 yellow onion, chopped
1 large potato, peeled and finely
  chopped
1 tsp. salt

Pick over beans and soak in water overnight. Rinse and drain.

Place soaked beans and all other ingredients in the slow cooker. Cover and cook on high heat until beans are tender, about 6 to 8 hours. Remove ham hock. Discard bone, skin and fat. Chop meat, return to soup and serve.

TEXAN BEAN AND SAUSAGE SOUP

Spicy chorizo sausage is used here, but you can also use kiel-basa-type sausage too. Just use ½ lb. of the kielbasa sausage, diced. No need to cook it; just add it with all the other ingredients. Try topping this soup with salsa, sour cream or slices of avocado.

1 cup dried black beans
½ lb. chorizo sausage
4 cups water
4 cups chicken stock
2 stalks celery, chopped

1 yellow onion, minced
1 cup commercially prepared
  salsa
½ tsp. ground cumin
1 tsp. salt

Pick over beans and soak in water overnight. Rinse and drain.

In a medium skillet, brown chorizo. Drain fat and place cooked sausage in the slow cooker. Add soaked beans and all remaining ingredients. Cover and cook on high heat until beans are tender, about 6 to 8 hours.

CAL-MEX BLACK BEAN SOUP

Many bean soups rely on ham, bacon and sausage for flavor, because the beans themselves aren't very flavorful. Here, a small amount of meat is used, but the soup gets a lot of its flavor from the herbs and vegetables. Top each bowl with a spoonful of sour cream or salsa.

4 cans (15 oz. each) black beans
1 can (15 oz.) refried black
   beans
2 yellow onions, minced
2 red bell peppers, chopped
2 cans (4 oz. each) mild green
   chiles, chopped
3 cloves garlic, minced

1 cup chopped cooked ham
8 cups stock, any kind, or water
1 tbs. ground cumin
1 tsp. freshly ground black
   pepper
$1/2$ cup minced fresh cilantro
2 tbs. brown sugar, packed

Combine all ingredients in the slow cooker. Stir to mix well. Cover and cook on low heat for 6 to 8 hours.

BARLEY AND PANCETTA SOUP

Pancetta (Italian bacon) is simmered with barley for a thick and hearty soup. Serve with a light green salad.

1/2 lb. pancetta, cut into tiny cubes
1 yellow onion, minced
1 cup minced celery
1 1/4 cups pearl barley
6 cups chicken stock
freshly grated Parmesan cheese, optional

In a medium saucepan, cook pancetta over medium heat for 5 minutes. Add onion, celery and barley and sauté until onion is translucent, about 10 minutes. Transfer all to the slow cooker.

Add stock to slow cooker and cover. Cook on low heat for 4 to 6 hours, or until barley is tender. Top with Parmesan cheese, if desired.

CHUNKY SPLIT PEA SOUP

Use either yellow or green split peas in this recipe — they both taste great. If the soup is really thick after the cooking time, add water (or chicken or vegetable stock), about 1/2 cup at a time, until you reach desired consistency. You can also use chicken stock or vegetable stock here.) Try topping this soup with crumbled, crisply-cooked bacon or grated cheddar cheese.

8 cups water
2 ham hocks
1 lb. split peas
2 carrots, cut into 1/4-inch thick slices

3 stalks celery, cut into 1/4-inch thick slices
1 yellow onion, chopped
1 large potato, peeled and chopped

Combine all ingredients in the slow cooker. Cover and cook on high heat until peas are soft and tender, about 4 to 6 hours.

Remove ham hock. Discard bone, skin and fat. Chop meat, return to soup and serve.

LENTIL AND BROWN RICE SOUP

Servings: 8–10

I like to serve this with a hearty "peasant-style" bread — and it goes well with a tall glass of very cold beer!

10 cups stock, any kind
2 cups lentils
2 carrots, chopped
1 yellow onion, chopped
2 stalks celery, chopped
1 can (14.5 oz.) tomatoes
1½ cups brown rice
1 lb. garlic sausage, chopped

Combine all ingredients in the slow cooker. Cook on high heat for 6 hours, or until brown rice is tender.

AUTUMN TURKEY SOUP

This is an ideal way to use a post-Thanksgiving turkey; the soup is a far cry from Thanksgiving tastes and textures. So when you are tired of reheating your leftover turkey and mashed potatoes, try this soup. If you can, make a stock using the turkey carcass. Just follow the recipe for chicken stock, using the turkey carcass instead. If you cannot find the tiny new potatoes called creamers, you can use red potatoes cut into 1/2-inch pieces.

4 cups chopped cooked turkey
8 cups chicken or turkey stock
4 cups shredded Swiss chard
1 lb. tiny red new potatoes
  ("creamers")

2 cups chopped carrots
2 cups chopped celery
2 cups chopped mushrooms
1/2 lb. banana squash, peeled
  and cut into 1-inch pieces

Combine all ingredients in the slow cooker. Cover and cook on low heat until all vegetables are tender, about 4 to 6 hours.

HAMBURGER VEGETABLE SOUP

Kids really like this simple vegetable soup — it has all the favorite kid vegetables, in a mild beef stock.

1 lb. lean ground beef
4 stalks celery, chopped
4 carrots, chopped
2 potatoes, peeled and chopped
1 cup frozen peas
1 cup frozen corn kernels
6 cups beef stock
$\frac{1}{2}$ tsp. dried oregano

In a medium skillet, brown ground beef over medium-high heat. Drain fat and place cooked beef in the slow cooker. Add all remaining ingredients and stir to mix. Cover and cook on low heat for 6 to 8 hours.

CHIPOTLE CHICKEN SOUP

These smoked jalapeño peppers are very hot, so use only ½ a pepper if you don't like your food too spicy. Top with broken corn chips and a spoonful of sour cream.

2 tbs. vegetable oil
2 boneless, skinless chicken
  breast halves
1 yellow onion, chopped
2 cloves garlic, minced
2 cups corn kernels, frozen

2 carrots, chopped
2 medium potatoes, peeled and
  chopped
6 cups chicken stock
1 chipotle pepper
½ tsp. salt

Heat oil in a medium skillet over medium heat. Add chicken and cook until brown on all sides. Remove from pan and set aside to cool slightly. When cool enough to handle, chop into small pieces and transfer to the slow cooker. Place onion and garlic in skillet and cook until onion begins to brown. Transfer to slow cooker. Add carrots, potatoes, stock, pepper and salt. Stir to mix. Cover and cook on low heat for 6 to 8 hours. Remove chipotle pepper prior to serving.

CHICKEN AND STARS SOUP

This comfort soup has the pasta added at the last moment, so the stars stay firm. The slow-cooked stock with tiny bits of vegetables will warm you on the coldest winter day.

8 cups chicken stock
2 cups finely chopped cooked chicken
4 carrots, finely chopped
1/2 yellow onion, minced
2 stalks celery, finely chopped
4 oz. uncooked pastina or stars

Combine all ingredients, except pasta, in the slow cooker. Stir to mix. Cover and cook on low heat for 6 to 8 hours.

Just prior to serving, cook pasta according to package directions. Drain pasta and add to soup. Serve immediately.

BAKED POTATO SOUP

Servings: 6–8

Next time you bake potatoes for dinner, throw a few more in, and you can have this wonderful soup the next day. I've always liked potatoes with skins on, and this method keeps the skins on the chunks of potato, instead of them separating.

6 large baked potatoes
1 cup chopped celery
1 yellow onion, minced
6 cups chicken stock
1 tsp. salt
2 cups half-and-half, or to taste

Cut potatoes into 1-inch chunks (do not peel). Place potatoes, celery, onion, chicken stock and salt in the slow cooker. Cover and cook on low heat for 6 to 8 hours. Lightly press potatoes to break them up a bit. Stir in half-and-half and heat through, about 15 minutes.

MANHATTAN CLAM CHOWDER

Some people are very adamant about which type is better, Manhattan (tomato-based) or Boston/New England (cream-based). Both can be easily made in the slow cooker. Here is the tomato-based soup.

4 slices bacon
1 yellow onion, chopped
2 stalks celery, minced
2 carrots, chopped
3 medium potatoes, peeled and chopped

1 bay leaf
1 can (28 oz.) stewed tomatoes, crushed
4 cups vegetable or fish stock
4 cans (6½ oz. each) clams, with juice

Brown bacon in a skillet over medium heat. Drain bacon and crumble. Add bacon to the slow cooker.

Add all remaining ingredients to slow cooker. Cover and cook on low heat for 8 hours. Remove bay leaf before serving.

NEW ENGLAND CLAM CHOWDER

Servings: 6–8

This creamy version of clam chowder has the cream added in the last hour of cooking so it will not curdle.

4 slices bacon
1 yellow onion, chopped
4 stalks celery, minced
3 medium potatoes, peeled and chopped
¼ cup chopped fresh parsley
2 cups vegetable or fish stock
4 cans (6½ oz. each) clams, with juice
4 cups half-and-half

Brown bacon in a skillet over medium heat. Drain bacon and crumble. Add bacon to the slow cooker.

Add all remaining ingredients, except half-and-half, to slow cooker. Cover and cook on low heat for 8 hours. Increase heat to high. Add half-and-half. Cook for 10 minutes to heat through.

SHRIMP RATATOUILLE

This has the flavors of ratatouille without all the vegetables. The sauce cooks slowly, and the shrimp are added at the end so they don't overcook. Serve with a simple rice pilaf.

1 yellow onion, chopped
3 cloves garlic, minced
2 bell peppers, any colors, seeded and chopped
2 cups peeled, seeded, chopped tomatoes

1 tsp. dried thyme
1 bay leaf
3 tbs. freshly squeezed lemon juice
2 lb. medium to large shrimp, peeled and deveined

Combine all ingredients except shrimp in the slow cooker. Cover and cook on low heat for 4 to 6 hours.

Add shrimp, stir to mix and replace lid. Continue cooking until shrimp are pink and firm, about 5 to 10 minutes, depending on size of shrimp. Remove bay leaf before serving.

BEEF CURRY WITH VEGETABLES

This is a very spicy curry, not sweet. Serve with some freshly baked bread and honey butter.

3 lb. beef stew meat
2 yellow onions, coarsely chopped
4 carrots, cut into 1-inch pieces
$1/4$ cup curry powder, or to taste
1 can (14 oz.) ready-cut tomatoes
2 cups beef stock
2 cups frozen green peas

Combine beef, onions, carrots, curry powder, tomatoes and stock in the slow cooker. Cover and cook on low heat for 8 to 10 hours, or high for 6 to 8 hours, until beef is fork-tender.

Add peas and stir to mix. Replace lid and cook for 15 minutes.

RICH BEEF STEW WITH GRAVY

Servings: 4–6

Here is a great way to make a stew with a rich, thick gravy — use a gravy mix! Be sure to cook this on low heat only, or else your gravy will stick to the slow cooker. Try using some different flavors of gravy mixes, such as onion or mushroom.

2 tbs. vegetable oil
2 lb. beef stew meat
1 cup red wine

2 cups water
1 pkg. (1.61 oz.) beef gravy mix
1/2 tsp. dried rosemary

Heat oil in a large skillet over medium-high heat. Add beef in batches and cook until well browned on all sides. Transfer cooked beef to the slow cooker.

When all beef has been browned, add wine to skillet to loosen browned bits from bottom of pan. In a small bowl, mix together beef stock and beef gravy mix, stirring until smooth. Add to wine in skillet and bring to a boil, stirring constantly. Add rosemary to gravy mixture and pour over beef in slow cooker.

Cook on low heat for 4 to 6 hours, or until beef is fork-tender.

STEAK AND MUSHROOM STEW

You can use cooked, leftover steak for this stew — just cook for a total of about 4 hours and skip browning the beef in butter.

¼ cup butter
2 lb. round steak, cut into 1-inch pieces
1 lb. mushrooms, sliced
½ cup sherry

1 yellow onion, chopped
¼ cup chopped fresh parsley
3 cups beef stock
1 bay leaf

Melt butter in a skillet over medium heat. Add beef in batches and cook until browned. Transfer browned beef to the slow cooker.

When done cooking beef, add mushrooms to skillet. Sauté until mushrooms' liquid is released and they begin to brown. Add sherry and scrape up any browned bits from bottom of pan. Pour sherry and mushrooms into slow cooker.

Add onion, parsley, stock and bay leaf to slow cooker. Cover and cook on high heat for 6 hours. Remove bay leaf before serving.

SWEET AND SMOKY BEEF STEW

Take the flavors of barbecue, slow cook them with beef, and you have this sweet and smoky stew. You can serve this on top of a big baked potato for a Saturday night feast.

2 tbs. vegetable oil
3 lb. beef stew meat
1 yellow onion, finely chopped
3 cloves garlic, minced
4 cups commercially prepared
   tomato-based salsa

2 cups beef stock
1/4 cup vinegar
1/2 cup brown sugar, packed
1/4 cup Worcestershire sauce
2 tsp. Liquid Smoke

Heat oil in a large skillet over medium heat. Add beef in batches and cook until browned. Transfer browned beef to the slow cooker.

Add all remaining ingredients to slow cooker. Cook on high heat for 6 to 8 hours, until beef is fall-apart tender.

PORK AND APPLE STEW

Pork and apples complement each other so well it seems a natural to cook them together. This stew is slightly sweet and perfect for autumn meals.

2 lb. pork stew meat
2 large green apples, cored and cut into quarters
$\frac{1}{2}$ cup chopped yellow onion
2 tbs. maple syrup
1 cup chicken stock
1 tbs. cornstarch
$\frac{1}{4}$ cup chicken stock

Place pork, apples, onion, maple syrup and 1 cup stock in the slow cooker. Stir to mix well. Cover and cook on low heat for 6 to 8 hours, or until pork is very tender. Raise slow cooker temperature to high. Mix cornstarch with $\frac{1}{4}$ cup stock until smooth. Add to stew, stirring constantly. Cook for 10 to 15 minutes, stirring frequently, until thickened.

CHICKEN WITH SUN-DRIED TOMATOES

Servings: 4–6

*Bits of intensely flavored tomatoes simmer with chicken and wine
for a simple Italian stew. Serve with wide egg noodles and a salad.*

2 tbs. olive oil
1 chicken, cut into serving pieces
2 cloves garlic, minced
1/2 cup white wine
1 1/2 cups chicken stock
1 tsp. dried basil
1/2 cup chopped sun-dried tomatoes, cut into slivers

Heat oil in a large skillet over medium-high heat. Add chicken
and brown on all sides. Transfer chicken to the slow cooker.

Add garlic, wine, stock and basil to skillet. Bring to a boil, scraping up any browned bits from bottom of pan. Pour over chicken in
slow cooker. Scatter sun-dried tomatoes over the top.

Cover and cook on low heat for 4 to 6 hours.

GARLIC CHICKEN

Yes, there is a lot of garlic in this recipe, but the slow cooking helps mellow the taste.

$^1/_2$ cup white wine
1 cup chicken stock
$^1/_2$ tsp. dried oregano
$^1/_2$ tsp. dried basil
1 chicken, cut into serving pieces
15 cloves garlic, peeled and cut in half
1 lb. tomatoes, coarsely chopped

Combine wine, stock, oregano and basil in the slow cooker. Add chicken to slow cooker. Scatter garlic over chicken and top with tomatoes. Cover and cook on low heat for 6 to 8 hours.

Remove chicken, garlic and tomatoes from slow cooker and set on a serving platter. If desired, reduce cooking liquid for use as a sauce by pouring liquid into a medium saucepan and cooking over high heat for 10 minutes.

CRAN-APPLE CHICKEN

The bright, tart flavor of cranberries is tempered by the addition of apples to this chicken dish. You can make this any time of year by using frozen cranberries instead of fresh.

6 chicken breast halves
1 cup fresh or frozen cranberries
1 green apple, peeled, cored and sliced
2 tbs. brown sugar, packed
1 cup apple juice or cider

Place chicken at the bottom of the slow cooker. Sprinkle cranberries and apples over chicken. Mix brown sugar and apple juice together and pour over chicken and fruit. Cover and cook on low heat for 6 to 8 hours.

FIREBALL CHILI

Yes, this is a hot and spicy chili. VERY hot and VERY spicy! Use 5 jalapeños if you want hot and spicy; use 10 for painfully hot. There are no beans here, either.

2 lb. hot chorizo sausage
2 lb. ground beef
3 yellow onions, chopped
2 cloves garlic, chopped
1 can (28 oz. can) tomatoes, crushed

2 cups beef stock
1 tbs. ground cumin
1 tbs. chili powder
5–10 jalapeño chile peppers, seeded and minced

If using chorizo in links, remove sausage meat from casings and discard casings. Place chorizo and beef in a large skillet and brown meats over medium-high heat. Drain fat and add meats to the slow cooker.

Add all remaining ingredients to slow cooker. Cook on high heat for 6 hours.

CHICKEN CHILI

Here, cubed chicken is cooked with traditional chili ingredients for a different version of chili. This makes a mild chili—you can adjust the heat by using regular or hot chili powder or a combination.

1/4 cup vegetable oil
4 boneless, skinless chicken breast halves
1 yellow onion, chopped
2 cloves garlic, minced
2 stalks celery, chopped
3 cans (14 oz. each) tomatoes, crushed

2 cans (15 oz. each) pinto beans
1 can (4 oz.) mild green chiles, chopped
1/4 cup chili powder
2 tsp. ground cumin
1/4 cup chopped fresh cilantro

Cut chicken breasts into small (1/2-inch) chunks. Heat oil in a large skillet over medium heat. Add chicken, in batches if necessary, and cook until lightly golden. Transfer cooked chicken to the slow cooker. Add all remaining ingredients and stir to mix well. Cook for 6 hours on high heat.

WHITE BEAN AND BASIL SOUP

Serve this Italian soup with grated Parmesan cheese or croutons.

1 lb. dried great Northern beans
1 yellow onion, minced
3 cloves garlic, minced
1 potato, peeled and chopped

6 cups chicken or vegetable stock
1 tsp. garlic salt
2 cups freshly chopped tomatoes
$1/4$ cup finely chopped fresh basil

Combine beans, onion, garlic, potato, stock and salt in the pressure cooker. Stir to mix well. Secure pressure cooker lid. Place over high heat and bring pressure up to high, about 15 minutes. Cook at high pressure for 35 minutes. Reduce pressure and release lid.

Stir in tomatoes and basil. Serve immediately.

SLOW COOKER METHOD

Soak beans overnight. Rinse and drain. Place beans, onion, garlic, potatoes, stock and salt in the slow cooker. Cover and cook over medium heat for 6 to 8 hours, until beans are tender. Stir in tomatoes and basil. Serve immediately.

REAL RUSSIAN BORSCHT

This hearty soup is close to a stew. The tiny bits of beef make this soup hearty. It is an excellent way to use up some leftover roast.

6 cups beef stock
2 cups minced cooked beef
1 cup shredded carrots
1 lb. beets, peeled and chopped
1½ cups shredded cabbage

1 yellow onion, minced
1 can (14 oz.) stewed tomatoes, crushed
1 bay leaf

Combine all ingredients in the pressure cooker. Stir to mix well. Secure pressure cooker lid. Place over high heat and bring pressure up to high. Cook at high pressure for 10 minutes. Reduce pressure and release lid. Remove bay leaf before serving.

STOVETOP METHOD

Combine all ingredients in a large stockpot. Stir to mix well. Bring to a boil over high heat, cover and reduce heat to low. Simmer for 30 to 45 minutes, stirring occasionally. Remove bay leaf and serve.

↘ RICE SOUP

Servings: 4–6

*:ooks so fast you'll never use canned chicken rice soup
your chicken breasts are slightly frozen, it will be easier to
↘ into thin strips and then into tiny pieces.*

1/2 cup uncooked white rice	1 yellow onion, minced
6 cups chicken stock	1 cup chopped celery
2 boneless, skinless chicken	2 carrots, chopped
breast halves, cut into pieces	1/2 tsp. salt

Combine all ingredients in the pressure cooker. Stir to mix well. Secure pressure cooker lid. Place over high heat and bring pressure up to high. Cook at high pressure for 10 minutes. Reduce pressure and release lid.

STOVETOP METHOD

Combine all ingredients in a stockpot. Stir to mix well. Bring to a boil over high heat and reduce heat to low. Cover and simmer until rice is tender, about 20 to 25 minutes.

VEGETARIAN CHILI

Servings: 6–8

This chili is a lot of beans and vegetables in a rich, spicy stock.

1 bell pepper, seeded and chopped
2 cups chopped mushrooms
2 zucchini, chopped
3 cloves garlic, minced
1 yellow onion, chopped
2½ cups dried pinto or black
  beans

2 tbs. vegetable oil
6 cups vegetable stock or water
1 tbs. chili powder
2 tsp. ground cumin
½ tsp. ground black pepper
1 tsp. garlic salt
1 can (15 oz.) puréed tomatoes

Combine all ingredients in a large (6-quart or more) pressure cooker. Mix well. Secure pressure cooker lid. Place over high heat and bring pressure up to high, about 15 minutes. Cook at high pressure for 45 minutes. Reduce pressure and release lid.

SLOW COOKER METHOD

Soak beans overnight. Rinse and drain beans. Combine all ingredients in the slow cooker. Cover and cook on high heat for 6 to 8 hours, until beans are tender.

OLD-FASHIONED PORK AND BEANS   Servings: 4–6 as a main dish

This can be a side dish with barbecue, or a meal in itself when served with a salad and some fresh hot cornbread.

1 lb. pinto beans
1 yellow onion, minced
10 cups water
1 cup light molasses or honey
2 tsp. salt

$\frac{1}{2}$ tsp. ground cloves
$\frac{1}{2}$ lb. salt pork, cut into $\frac{1}{2}$-inch
  cubes
2 tbs. vegetable oil

Combine all ingredients in a large (6 quart or more) pressure cooker. Mix well. Secure pressure cooker lid.

Place over high heat and bring to high pressure. Cook at high pressure for 45 minutes. Reduce pressure and release lid.

SLOW COOKER METHOD

Soak beans overnight. Rinse and drain beans. Combine all ingredients in the slow cooker. Cover and cook on high heat for 6 to 8 hours, until beans are tender.

CREOLE CHICKEN

If you like a bit of heat to your Creole foods, increase the amount of hot pepper sauce to taste.

2 tbs. vegetable oil
1 chicken, cut into 4–6 pieces
1 yellow onion, chopped
3 stalks celery, coarsely chopped
1 green bell pepper, chopped
2 cloves garlic, minced

$\frac{1}{2}$ tsp. dried thyme
$\frac{1}{2}$ tsp. dried basil
$\frac{1}{2}$ tsp. Tabasco Sauce
1 cup chicken stock
2 cups freshly chopped tomatoes
1 cup sliced okra, optional

Combine all ingredients in the pressure cooker. Secure pressure cooker lid. Place over high heat and bring to high pressure. Cook at high pressure for 8 minutes. Reduce pressure and release lid.

STOVETOP METHOD

Heat oil in a large skillet over medium heat. Add chicken and cook until browned on all sides. Add all remaining ingredients. Mix well. Cover and simmer over low heat for 30 minutes.

4-SPICE CHICKEN CURRY

Servings: 6

This curry is not made with commercially prepared curry powder, but a simple 4-spice blend.

6 chicken breasts, cut into 2-inch pieces
2 yellow onions, cut into large chunks
1 can (15 oz.) whole baby corn
3 carrots, cut into 2-inch pieces
1½ tsp. ground cumin
2 tsp. ground coriander
½ tsp. ground ginger
1 tsp. ground turmeric
2 cups chicken stock
½ tsp. salt

Combine all ingredients in a large pressure cooker. Mix well. Secure pressure cooker cover. Place over high heat and bring to high pressure. Cook at high pressure for 9 minutes. Reduce pressure and release lid.

SLOW COOKER METHOD

Combine all ingredients in the slow cooker. Cover and cook on low heat for 4 to 6 hours.

CALIFORNIA-STYLE FISH STEW

This light fish stew works well in a pressure cooker, because the fish cooks quickly without breaking apart.

1 lb. halibut, cod or pollock	½ tsp. dried basil
¼ cup white wine	3 stalks celery, cut into chunks
2 tbs. fresh squeezed lemon juice	1 yellow onion, chopped
2 cloves garlic, minced	1 cup sliced mushrooms
½ cup chopped fresh flat-leaf parsley	2 cups fish or vegetable stock

Cut fish into 6 or 8 pieces. Place all ingredients in the pressure cooker. Secure lid on pressure cooker. Place over high heat and bring to high pressure. Cook at high pressure for 4 minutes. Reduce pressure and release lid.

STOVETOP METHOD

Place all ingredients in a large stockpot. Cover and bring to a boil over high heat. Reduce heat to low and simmer for 10 minutes.

BEEF STEW PROVENÇAL

You can have all the flavors of a slow-cooked French stew in about half an hour. Serve with some parsley potatoes and red wine.

3 lb. beef stew meat
2 cups red wine
2 cloves garlic, minced
1 tsp. dried thyme
1 tsp. dried rosemary

3 anchovy fillets, minced
$\frac{1}{2}$ tsp. salt
2 carrots, cut into 2-inch pieces
1 yellow onion, cut into chunks
$\frac{1}{2}$ cup chopped, pitted olives

Combine all ingredients in the pressure cooker and stir to mix. Secure lid on pressure cooker. Place over high heat and bring to high pressure. Cook on high pressure for 15 minutes. Let pressure drop naturally (about 10 to 15 minutes) and release lid. If beef is not fork-tender, replace lid, bring to high pressure again and cook for another 5 minutes. Let pressure drop naturally before opening.

SLOW COOKER METHOD

Combine all ingredients in the slow cooker. Cover and cook on low heat for 8 hours, until beef is fork-tender.

PEASANT POTATO SOUP

This version of potato soup is not puréed but has bits of potato in a slightly thickened stock.

3 medium potatoes, peeled and diced
1 carrot, chopped
½ yellow onion, minced
2 medium tomatoes, chopped

2 cups finely chopped garlic sausage or kielbasa
3 tbs. butter
3 tbs. flour
8 cups beef or chicken stock

Heat oven to 400°. Place potatoes, carrot, onion, tomatoes and garlic sausage in a large, covered casserole dish or Dutch oven.

In a medium saucepan, melt butter over medium heat. Add flour and whisk until smooth. Add stock, stirring constantly. Bring stock to a boil and cook for 5 minutes. Pour hot stock mixture over vegetables in casserole dish. Cover and bake for 90 minutes.

CURRIED LENTIL SOUP

This is a very filling soup without meat. You can also use vegetable stock for a vegetarian version

2 russet potatoes, peeled and chopped
2 carrots, peeled and chopped
2 stalks celery, chopped
12 oz. lentils
2 cloves garlic, minced
8 cups chicken or beef stock
2 tbs. curry powder
1 tsp. salt

Heat oven to 400°. Combine all ingredients in a large, covered casserole dish. Cover and bake for 1 hour, or until lentils and potatoes are very tender.

GREEN CHILE CHICKEN

Mild green chiles and tomatoes make a sauce for this chicken stew. This dish is Mexican in flavor but very mild, with minimal heat.

1/4 cup vegetable oil
1 chicken, cut into serving pieces
2 cloves garlic, minced
1 can (28 oz.) tomatoes
2 cans (4 oz. each) mild green chiles, chopped
1 tbs. ground cumin
1/2 cup white wine

Heat oven to 375°. Heat oil in a large skillet over medium heat. Add chicken and cook until browned on all sides. Transfer chicken to a covered casserole dish or 9-x-13-inch baking dish.

In a medium bowl, mix together garlic, tomatoes, chiles, cumin and wine. Pour over chicken. Use a lid or foil to cover and bake for 1 hour, or until chicken is tender.

BEANS AND BACON

When you have lots of bacon and vegetables surrounding the beans, this is more than just a side dish. I like to use a light-tasting beer, but feel free to use your favorite.

½ lb. bacon
1 yellow onion, finely chopped
1 jalapeño chile pepper, seeded
   and minced
5 cups water
1 lb. pinto or black beans

1 bottle (12 oz.) beer
1 cup finely chopped celery
1 cup chopped tomatoes
1 cup frozen or canned corn
   kernels

Heat oven to 350°. Fry bacon in a medium skillet until crisp. Drain all but 2 tbs. of the fat from skillet and add onion and jalapeño pepper. Sauté until onion is translucent, about 5 minutes.

Crumble bacon into a large, covered casserole dish. Add cooked onion, pepper, water, beans, beer, celery, tomatoes and corn to casserole. Stir to mix. Cover and bake for 3 hours, or until beans are tender and most of liquid has been absorbed.

CRAB AND SHRIMP JAMBALAYA

Servings: 4–6

If you are from the south, please forgive this California version of jambalaya. A more traditional New Orleans jambalaya would be made with pork, chicken and seafood.

2 tbs. butter
1 cup long-grain rice
1 clove garlic, minced
½ cup diced celery
½ cup chopped green bell
   pepper

2 cups water or vegetable, fish or
   chicken stock
1½ cups ready-cut tomatoes
½ lb. cooked lump crabmeat
½ lb. cooked shrimp or prawns
½ tsp. salt

Heat oven to 350°. In a skillet, melt butter over medium heat. Add rice and garlic and sauté until rice becomes translucent.

Place sautéed rice in a covered casserole dish. Add all remaining ingredients and gently stir to mix. Cover and bake until rice is tender, about 45 minutes.

VEAL IN WINE

This stew is perfect for a special party. Since you don't have to watch it closely, you can relax while it cooks. The white wine sauce the veal cooks in is elegant but easy to make.

2 tbs. butter	2 cups white wine
1 yellow onion, chopped	2 carrots, thickly sliced
1 clove garlic, minced	1 tsp. dried thyme
2 lb. veal chunks, cut into about	1 tsp. salt
1½-inch pieces	

Heat oven to 350°. Heat butter in a medium saucepan over medium heat. Add onion and garlic and sauté until they begin to brown. Add veal to pan and cook until meat is lightly browned. Add wine and stir to loosen any browned bits on bottom of pan.

Place veal and wine mixture in a covered casserole dish. Add remaining ingredients, cover and bake for 1½ to 2 hours or until meat is tender.

SUNDAY NIGHT BEEF STEW

This has everything in it; beef, rich gravy, ve
on top. You don't need anything else for a full

2 lb. beef stew meat
1 yellow onion, chopped
2 carrots, cut into 1-inch chunks
2 stalks celery, cut into 1-inch chunks
2 medium potatoes, peeled and cut into 1-inch ...
½ cup fresh or frozen green peas
1 cup ready-cut tomatoes
2 cups beef stock
1 container refrigerated biscuit dough

Heat oven to 400°. Combine all ingredients, except biscuit dough, in a large covered casserole dish. Cover and bake for 2 to 2½ hours, until beef is very tender.

Place biscuits on top of stew and return to oven. Bake for another 10 minutes, or until biscuits are golden and done.

LENTIL STEW

*...ew has an "old-world" taste and texture; a course, coun-
...e bread is perfect for soaking up the tasty stock.*

...b. lamb stew meat
2 cups lentils
3 cups beef stock
1 yellow onion, chopped
1 clove garlic, minced
1 cup chopped celery
1 cup ready-cut tomatoes

Heat oven to 450°. Combine all ingredients in a large, covered casserole dish and bake for 1 hour. Check stew and add more stock if needed. Reduce heat to 350° and bake for another 60 to 90 minutes, until lamb is tender.

PORK CURRY

Sweet potatoes are a surprise ingredient in this curry. The sweetness of the potatoes goes well with the spicy curry sauce.

3 lb. pork stew meat
6 cups chicken stock
2 cloves garlic, minced
1 tsp. ground allspice
3 tbs. curry powder
$\frac{1}{2}$ tsp. cinnamon
1 yellow onion, sliced
3 large sweet potatoes, peeled and cut into 1-inch chunks
3 carrots, cut into 1-inch chunks
1 cup frozen or fresh green peas

Heat oven to 375°. In a large skillet, brown pork in batches if necessary. Place browned meat in a large Dutch oven or covered casserole dish. Add all remaining ingredients and stir to mix. Cover and bake for 2 hours.

INDEX